Instant Drools Starter

The ultimate Starter guide for evaluating rules engines
and getting started with Drools

Jeremy Ary

BIRMINGHAM - MUMBAI

Instant Drools Starter

First published: March 2013

Production Reference: 1200313

Published by Packt Publishing Ltd.
Livery Place
35 Livery Street
Birmingham B3 2PB, UK.

ISBN 978-1-78216-554-5

www.packtpub.com

Credits

Author

Jeremy Ary

Reviewer

Edson Tirelli

Acquisition Editor

Akram Hussain

Commissioning Editor

Maria D'souza

Technical Editor

Chirag Jani

Project Coordinator

Sneha Modi

Proofreader

Maria Gould

Graphics

Aditi Gajjar

Production Coordinator

Prachali Bhiwandkar

Cover Work

Prachali Bhiwandkar

Cover Image

Conidon Miranda

About the Author

Jeremy Ary is a Senior Software Developer, born and raised in Tennessee, US. He began working with Drools systems over five years ago, and became active in the community and conferences, furthering his curiosity and desire to work with rules engines. He has spent his time in the field improving various rule-based legacy systems in the financial field and creating others from scratch that automated company workflow processes. He's also authored highly-scalable rule-based emergency response and notification systems for both domestic and international customers.

When not in code monkey mode, Jeremy can be found in his shop doing woodworking, out on the waters fishing, or at home spending time with his two dachshunds, his loving wife Becca, and his newborn son Everett.

You can keep up with Jeremy's latest works at his Github account, `www.github.com/jeremyary`, or you can reach out to him via LinkedIn at `www.linkedin.com/in/jeremyary/` or e-mail him at `jeremy.ary@gmail.com`.

About the Reviewer

Edson Tirelli is a Principal Software Engineer at Red Hat and the Drools Project Lead. He has more than 10 years of experience in enterprise software development and has been working on the design and development of the Drools project for more than six years. His main interests are general AI research, complex event processing (CEP), decision management, knowledge representation, languages, and compilers.

www.packtpub.com

Support files, eBooks, discount offers and more

You might want to visit www.packtpub.com for support files and downloads related to your book.

Did you know that Packt offers eBook versions of every book published, with PDF and ePub files available? You can upgrade to the eBook version at www.packtpub.com and as a print book customer, you are entitled to a discount on the eBook copy. Get in touch with us at service@packtpub.com for more details.

At www.packtpub.com, you can also read a collection of free technical articles, sign up for a range of free newsletters and receive exclusive discounts and offers on Packt books and eBooks.

packtlib.packtpub.com

Do you need instant solutions to your IT questions? PacktLib is Packt's online digital book library. Here, you can access, read and search across Packt's entire library of books.

Why Subscribe?

- ✦ Fully searchable across every book published by Packt
- ✦ Copy and paste, print and bookmark content
- ✦ On demand and accessible via web browser

Free Access for Packt account holders

If you have an account with Packt at www.packtpub.com, you can use this to access PacktLib today and view nine entirely free books. Simply use your login credentials for immediate access.

This book is dedicated to my son, Everett. Always be true to who you are, son, don't spend your life trying to become someone you aren't. Nobody does you better than you!

Table of Contents

Instant Drools Starter

Welcome to *Drools Starter*. This book has been especially created to provide you with all the information that you need to get started with Drools. You will learn the basics of Drools, get started with building your first rule system, and learn core functions and helpful tips and tricks when it comes to using Drools in your applications.

This book contains the following sections:

So, what is Drools? will tell you what Drools actually is, what a Business Rule Management System such as Drools can do for you, when you should and shouldn't choose a rule engine, and why Drools is a great choice.

Installation will teach you how to integrate Drools into a new or existing Java project with minimum hassle in order to get you writing and evaluating rules as soon as possible.

Quick start will break down the basics and show you how to perform one of the core tasks associated with Drools Expert: writing and applying a simple rule file using the Drools Rule Language.

Top 5 features you need to know about will show you how to perform four tasks with the most important features of the Drools core rule engine. By the end of this section you will be able to read and write basic rules in Drools Rule Language syntax, work with facts (objects fed to the rule engine), test your rules, debug the rule evaluation process, and name the five core modules of Drools and briefly explain their purposes.

People and places you should get to know will provide you with many useful links to project documentation and mailing lists, as well as a number of helpful articles, tutorials, blogs, and the Twitter feeds of Drools' super contributors.

So, what is Drools?

The techie answer guaranteed to get that glazed over look from anyone hounding you for details on project design is that Drools, part of the JBoss Enterprise BRMS product since federating in 2005, is a **Business Rule Management System (BRMS)** and rules engine written in Java which implements and extends the Rete pattern-matching algorithm within a rules engine capable of both forward and backward chaining inference.

Now, how about an answer fit for someone new to rules engines? After all, you're here to learn the basics, right? Drools is a collection of tools which allow us to separate and reason over logic and data found within business processes. Ok, but what does that mean? Digging deeper, the keywords in that statement we need to consider are "logic" and "data".

Logic, or *rules* in our case, are pieces of knowledge often expressed as, "*When* some conditions occur, *then* do some tasks". Simple enough, no? These pieces of knowledge could be about any process in your organization, such as how you go about approving TPS reports, calculate interest on a loan, or how you divide workload among employees. While these processes sound complex, in reality, they're made up of a collection of simple business rules. Let's consider a daily ritual process for many workers: the morning coffee. The whole process is second nature to coffee drinkers. As they prepare for their work day, they probably don't consider the steps involved—they simply react to situations at hand. However, we can capture the process as a series of simple rules:

+ *When* your mug is dirty, *then* go clean it
+ *When* your mug is clean, *then* go check for coffee
+ *When* the pot is full, *then* pour yourself a cup and return to your desk
+ *When* the pot is empty, *then* mumble about co-workers and make some coffee

Alright, so that's logic, but what's data? *Facts* (our word for data) are the objects that drive the decision process for us. Given the rules from our coffee example, some facts used to drive our decisions would be the mug and the coffee pot. While we know from reading our rules what to do when the mug or pot are in a particular state, we need facts that reflect an actual state on a particular day to reason over.

In seeing how a BRMS allows us to define the business rules of a business process, we can now state some of the features of a rules engine. As stated before, we've separated logic from data—always a good thing! In our example, notice how we didn't see any detail about how to clean our mug or how to make a new batch of coffee, meaning we've also separated *what to do* from *how to do it*, thus allowing us to change procedure without altering logic. Lastly, by gathering all of our rules in one place, we've centralized our business process knowledge. This gives us an excellent facility when we need to explain a business process or transfer knowledge. It also helps to prevent tribal knowledge, or the ownership and understanding of an undocumented procedure by just one or a few users.

So when is a BRMS the right choice?

- ✦ Consider a rules engine when a problem is too complex for traditional coding approaches. Rules can abstract away the complexity and prevent usage of fragile implementations.

- ✦ Rules engines are also beneficial when a problem isn't fully known. More often than not, you'll find yourself iterating business methodology in order to fully understand small details involved that are second nature to users.

- ✦ Rules are flexible and allow us to easily change what we know about a procedure to accommodate this iterative design. This same flexibility comes in handy if you find that your logic changes often over time.

- ✦ Lastly, in providing a straightforward approach in documenting business rules, rules engines are an excellent choice if you find domain knowledge readily available, but via non-technical people who may be incapable of contributing to code.

Sounds great, so let's get started, right? Well, I promised I'd also help you decide when a rules engine is not the right choice for you. In using a rules engine, someone must translate processes into actual rules, which can be a blessing in taking business logic away from developers, but also a curse in required training. Secondly, if your logic doesn't change very often, then rules might be overkill. Likewise, If your project is small in nature and likely to be used once and forgotten, then rules probably aren't for you. However, beware of the small system that will grow in complexity going forward!

So if rules are right for you, why should you choose Drools? First and foremost, Drools has the flexibility of an open source license with the support of JBoss available. Drools also boasts five modules (to be discussed in more detail later), making their system quite extensible with domain-specific languages, graphical editing tools, web-based tools, and more. If you're partial to Eclipse, you'll also likely come to appreciate their plugin. Still not convinced? Read on and give it a shot—after all, that's why you're here, right?

Installation

In just five easy steps, you can integrate Drools into a new or existing project.

Step 1 – what do I need?

For starters, you will need to check that you have all of the required elements, listed as follows (all versions are as of time of writing):

+ Java 1.5 (or higher) SE JDK.

+ Apache Maven 3.0.4.

+ Eclipse 4.2 (Juno) and the Drools plugin.

+ Memory—512 MB (minimum), 1 GB or higher recommended. This will depend largely on the scale of your JVM and rule sessions, but the more the better!

Step 2 – installing Java

Java is the core language on which Drools is built, and is the language in which we'll be writing, so we'll definitely be needing that. The easiest way to get Java going is to download from and follow the installation instructions found at:

```
www.oracle.com/technetwork/java/javase/downloads/index.html
```

Step 3 – installing Maven

Maven is a build automation tool from Apache that lets us describe a configuration of the project we're building and leave dependency management (amongst other things) up to it to work out. Again, the easiest way to get Maven up and running is to download and follow the documentation provided with the tool, found at:

```
maven.apache.org/download.cgi
```

Step 4 – installing Eclipse

If you happen to have some other IDE of choice, or maybe you're just the old school type, then it's perfectly acceptable to author and execute your Drools-integrated code in your usual fashion. However, if you're an Eclipse fan, or you'd like to take advantage of auto-complete, syntax highlighting, and debugging features, then I recommend you go ahead and install Eclipse and the Drools plugin.

The version of Eclipse that we're after is Eclipse IDE for Java Developers, which you can download and find installation instructions for on their site:

```
www.eclipse.org/downloads/
```

Step 5 – installing the Drools Eclipse plugin

In order to add the IDE plugin to Eclipse, the easiest method is to use Eclipse's built-in update manager. First, you'll need to add something the plugin depends on—the **Graphical Editing Framework (GEF)**.

In the Eclipse menu, click on **Help**, then on **Install New Software...**, enter the following URL in the **Work with:** field, and hit **Add**:

```
download.eclipse.org/tools/gef/updates/releases/
```

Give your repository a nifty name in the pop-up window, such as GEF, and continue on with the install as prompted. You'll be asked to verify what you're installing and accept the license.

Now we can add the Drools plugin itself—you can find the URL you'll need by visiting:

```
www.jboss.org/drools/downloads.html
```

Then, search for the text `Eclipse update site` and you'll see the link you need. Copy the address of the link to your clipboard, head back into Eclipse, and follow the same process you did for installing GEF. Note that you'll be asked to confirm the install of unsigned content, and that this is expected.

And that's it!

By this point, you should be ready to integrate Drools into your applications. If you find yourself stuck, one of the good parts about an open source community is that there's nearly always someone who has faced your problem before and likely has a solution to recommend. Check towards the back of the book for a list of resources that can help get you going again!

Quick start – creating your first rules application

For the purposes of this book, we'll continue using Apache Maven for project structure management, given that Drools already relies on this tool and learning a bit about it may assist you in navigating the Drools source code. However, we'll begin with creating a new project with Eclipse and the Drools plugin. While this will not provide you with a Maven-enabled project or reflect what you'll typically find in an enterprise development structure, it does provide you with the basics needed to start tinkering with rules right away.

Step 1 – creating a Drools project with the Eclipse plugin

First things first, let's start a new project using the plugin's Drools Project Wizard to get things up and going.

1. Select **Project...** by navigating to **File | New**.

2. Expand the **Drools** folder and select **Drools Project**, then hit **Next**.

3. Give your new project a name such as `TacoShop`, and hit **Next**.

4. In this screen, the default settings are fine, but I wanted to point out a few things the wizard is capable of that we're not going to use. Leave the top two boxes checked only, but take note of the other options. Hit **Next**.

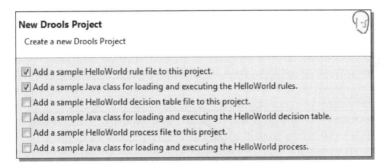

5. Since this is the first time you've created a Drools project, you're unlikely to have a Drools runtime environment created, as reflected by the warning, so let's do that now. Click on the blue link named **Configure Workspace Settings...**.

6. At this screen, click on **Add**, and then on the **Create a new Drools 5 Runtime...** button.

7. Specify a location for the plugin to place your JAR files.

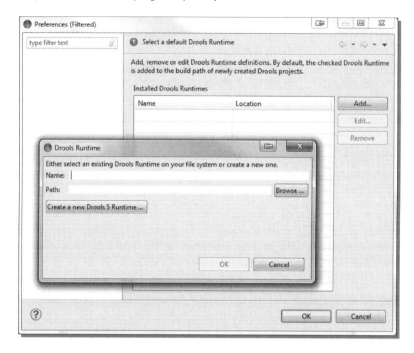

8. Back at the runtime screen, place a check next to the newly created Drools runtime location and hit **OK**.

9. Now click on **Finish** and let the plugin do its thing.

Congratulations! You've now got a working rules application. If you're in a hurry to see what DRL, or the Drools Rule Language, looks like, you can navigate to `Sample.drl` and have a look. You'll find the executable portion of code inside the file called `DroolsTest.java`. You can run it and see the output in your console by right-clicking the file name and selecting **Run As | Java Application**.

Checking your console, you should now see two lines of output. The first reads **Hello World**, and the second reads **Goodbye cruel world**. If you're seeing both, then it's a success! You've just set up and executed your first rules-integrated application.

Downloading the example code

You can download the example code files for all Packt books you have purchased from your account at `http://www.packtpub.com`. If you purchased this book elsewhere, you can visit `http://www.packtpub.com/support` and register to have the files e-mailed directly to you.

Step 2 – creating a new rules-enabled Maven project from scratch

The creation wizard cranked out a lot of code for us, and if we were to just continue on with this project, we'd be omitting explanation of the most vital parts of the code, so let's build up our own project piece by piece and find out what makes it tick.

We'll be creating a simple rules system that will aid us in rewarding customers of our fictional company, Tucker's Taco Shop, for large purchases and combo deals.

In a new or existing Maven project, let's add the required drools dependencies. I've created a new project called `DiscountProgram`. Your `pom.xml` file should look something like this:

```xml
<?xml version="1.0" encoding="UTF-8"?>
<project xmlns="maven.apache.org/POM/4.0.0"
         xmlns:xsi="www.w3.org/2001/XMLSchema-instance"
         xsi:schemaLocation="maven.apache.org/POM/4.0.0 maven.apache.
org/xsd/maven-4.0.0.xsd">
    <modelVersion>4.0.0</modelVersion>

        <groupId>com.tacoshop</groupId>
        <artifactId>DiscountProgram</artifactId>
    <version>0.0.1-SNAPSHOT</version>

    <properties>
        <droolsVersion>5.5.0.Final</droolsVersion>
    </properties>

    <dependencies>

        <dependency>
            <groupId>org.drools</groupId>
            <artifactId>drools-compiler</artifactId>
            <version>${droolsVersion}</version>
        </dependency>
        <dependency>
            <groupId>junit</groupId>
            <artifactId>junit</artifactId>
            <version>4.11</version>
            <scope>test</scope>
        </dependency>
        <dependency>
            <groupId>commons-lang</groupId>
            <artifactId>commons-lang</artifactId>
```

```
            <version>2.6</version>
        </dependency>
    </dependencies>
</project>
```

So what have we done here? We've specified some information about our project, mainly the `groupId`, `artifactId`, and version number—all things that Maven uses to identify your application. Secondly, we've added a property called `droolsVersion` to keep life simple so that we can't accidentally forget to change one of the Drools component version numbers in the future. Next, we've included the three main JAR files we'll need to utilize the Drools rules engine. The first is the `drools-compiler` dependency. It's worth mentioning here that by including `drools-compiler`, we've pulled two transitive dependencies worthy of noting, `knowledge-api` and `drools-core`. When the time comes to start digging into drools code, you'll see these API names again. Lastly, we've included `commons-lang`, another required dependency, and `junit` at the test scope level, to provide some mechanism to run our rules.

Step 3 – defining our rules and facts

Before we go much further, let's stop and think up a basic set of rules we'd like to include in our discount program. Let's allow customers a discount of 10 percent on purchases over $15. Let's also give 15 percent off for purchases over $25. Finally, we'll allow a combo deal discount of an additional 5 percent off for purchases containing two or more tacos and at least one drink. Remember, rules tend to follow the format of *When...then*, so let's word them as such:

+ *When* a customer makes a purchase greater than $15, *then* provide a 10 percent discount

+ *When* a customer makes a purchase greater than $25, *then* provide a 15 percent discount

+ *When* a customer makes a purchase containing two or more tacos and at least one drink, *then* provide an additional 5 percent discount

Now that we know what rules we'll have, let's figure out what facts we need to know about. Since we're intentionally sticking to a simple rule set, we only need to know about one thing, the purchase; we need to know how much it costs, what it consisted of, and the discount total.

Step 4 – translating facts into a data model

With a fact model in mind, we need to create a **Plain Old Java Object** (**POJO**) class to represent our model.

1. Create a new class which will represent the `Purchase` object.

2. Add properties to our class for each trait that we've deemed important to us.

3. Add getters and setters for said properties.

```
package com.tacoshop;

import java.math.BigDecimal;

public class Purchase {

  private BigDecimal total;

  private int tacoCount;

  private boolean drinkIncluded;

  private double discount;

  public Purchase(BigDecimal total, int tacoCount, boolean
drinkIncluded) {
    this.total = total;
    this.tacoCount = tacoCount;
    this.drinkIncluded = drinkIncluded;
    this.discount = 0;
  }

  public BigDecimal getTotal() {
    return total;
  }

  public void setTotal(BigDecimal total) {
    this.total = total;
  }

  public int getTacoCount() {
    return tacoCount;
  }

  public void setTacoCount(int tacoCount) {
    this.tacoCount = tacoCount;
  }

  public boolean isDrinkIncluded() {
    return drinkIncluded;
  }

  public void setDrinkIncluded(boolean drinkIncluded) {
```

```
    this.drinkIncluded = drinkIncluded;
  }

  public double getDiscount() {
    return discount;
  }

  public void setDiscount(double discount) {
    this.discount = discount;
  }
}
```

Nothing too out of the ordinary in there. We've got a simple POJO with a constructor, some properties, and their getters and setters. Moving along!

Step 5 – translating rules into Drools Rule Language

So we've established a data model and we've already defined what rules we need, so now let's build our DRL file.

1. Create a new file in `src/main/rules` called `discountRules.drl`. I've used a package called `com.tacoshop.rules` inside my rules file.

2. If you're using the Eclipse plugin, you can take advantage of their **Rule Resource** wizard by navigating to **New | Other... | Drools | Rule Resource**.

3. Add the following to your new rules file and save it:

```
package com.tacoshop.rules

import com.tacoshop.Purchase

rule "purchase over 15 and less than 25 dollars"
when
  $p : Purchase ( total > 15, total <= 25 )
then
  $p.setDiscount(0.10);
  System.out.println("Level 1 discount: " + $p.getDiscount());
end

rule "purchase over 25 dollars"
when
  $p : Purchase ( total > 25 )
then
  $p.setDiscount(0.15);
  System.out.println("Level 2 discount: " + $p.getDiscount());
end
```

```
rule "purchase contains combo" salience -1
when
  $p : Purchase ( drinkIncluded, tacoCount >= 2 )
then
  $p.setDiscount($p.getDiscount() + 0.05);
  System.out.println("Combo discount: " + $p.getDiscount());
end
```

Now let's break it down...hey, stop dancing, that's not what I meant. The rules! The package and import statements, as seen here at the top of the file, are structured the same way as they are in Java class files. The rules, however, aren't so familiar to us. Notice that each starts with a rule name, and follows the format of when ... then ... end. We've discussed something similar to that construct once or twice by now, right? It's all coming together.

Our rule *conditions* (the when bit) use a dialect called **MVFLEX Expression Language (MVEL)**, which makes them seem a little foreign to us. For one, we're not calling getters to access properties. MVEL takes care of that for us. It helps to read each condition aloud to yourself:

```
$p : Purchase ( total > 25 )
```

The previous code can be read aloud as "There exists some purchase having a total greater than 25." In the case that such a purchase is found, we set it to a variable, $p. In the *consequences* of our rules, we take some action desired when our condition is met. Notice the consequences in the rules look like Java, but also reference the $p variable set from the conditions. In our first rule consequence, we set a discount of 10 percent to $p and we print something to the console showing us that the discount has been added. The rest of the rules follow the same format. Feel free to take a moment to look them over and read them aloud. The last thing I should mention before we move on is the keyword seen on the combo rule, salience. This keyword sets priority to a rule. By default, all rules have a salience of zero. You can specify a negative or positive salience, so in our case, we've used a negative one. Why? Because we want our combo discount to be in addition to any other discounts added to the order, so we need to give it a lower priority to ensure it's done last.

Step 6 – doing something with our rules

Take a quick break, maybe grab some coffee (try not to think about coffee rules, it's a break). This is going to be a big one. I'll wait here.

Moving on! So now that we have a data model and a proper rule resource, we can get to executing our rules. We're going to create a JUnit test that will compile our rules, build a session, insert some facts, and fire our rules. Let's get started by taking a look at the whole test, then we can examine the contents:

```
@Test
  public void testRules() {

    StatefulKnowledgeSession session = null;
```

```
    try {
        KnowledgeBuilder builder = KnowledgeBuilderFactory.
newKnowledgeBuilder();
        builder.add(ResourceFactory.newClassPathResource("discountRules.
drl"), ResourceType.DRL);
        if (builder.hasErrors()) {
            throw new RuntimeException(builder.getErrors().toString());
        }

        KnowledgeBase knowledgeBase = KnowledgeBaseFactory.
newKnowledgeBase();
        knowledgeBase.addKnowledgePackages(builder.
getKnowledgePackages());

        session = knowledgeBase.newStatefulKnowledgeSession();

        // purchase > $15 and <= $25
        Purchase firstPurchase = new Purchase(new BigDecimal("16"), 1,
false);
        FactHandle purchaseFact = session.insert(firstPurchase);
            session.fireAllRules();

    } catch(Throwable t) {
        t.printStackTrace();
    } finally {
    if (session != null) {
        session.dispose();
      }
    }
}
```

Let's start at the top! We've made a standard JUnit test (for now, let's ignore the fact that we're not really asserting anything inside our test—we'll get to that later):

```
@Test
    public void testRules() {
```

It's good practice to wrap your rules code in a try/catch block. For that reason, we've extracted a variable declaration needed within the `finally` block to outside of the `try` block:

```
        StatefulKnowledgeSession session = null;
```

Let's talk a bit about what `StatefulKnowledgeSession` is. Our session is the main means of communication with the rules engine. It provides us with some handy methods for inserting, updating, and retracting our facts. It also gives us methods for setting global variables (more on these later), as well as a method I like to refer to as the Big Red Button, `fireAllRules()`.

Whenever you work with a session, it's important to always remember to use the `dispose()` function to dispose of it when you're done. If you don't, the garbage collector won't be able to free up the resources for you, and that means problems. The purpose of our `finally` block is to ensure that won't be an issue. So how do we build a session? Let's start with `KnowledgeBuilder`:

```
try {
    KnowledgeBuilder builder = KnowledgeBuilderFactory.
newKnowledgeBuilder();
    builder.add(ResourceFactory.newClassPathResource("discountRules.
drl"), ResourceType.DRL);
    if (builder.hasErrors()) {
     throw new RuntimeException(builder.getErrors().toString());
    }
```

What's happening here is the compilation of our rules resource. The `KnowledgeBuilder` is responsible for taking resources and compiling them into rule packages. If we have any syntax or other compilation errors within our rules (notice I didn't say logic!), now's the time that they'd show up. Once it's built, we'll need to do something with our nifty rule package. Moving on to `KnowledgeBase`:

```
KnowledgeBase knowledgeBase = KnowledgeBaseFactory.
newKnowledgeBase();
    knowledgeBase.addKnowledgePackages(builder.getKnowledgePackages());
```

Notice that `KnowledgeBase` accepts the packages created by our builder. The `KnowledgeBase` can be thought of as a manager for our collection of knowledge packages, or as I've been referring to it, rule packages. It primarily provides us with an interface for inserting and removing packages, as well as a method for creating sessions populated with our rule information:

```
session = knowledgeBase.newStatefulKnowledgeSession();
```

So now we have a rule session loaded up with our logic. Next it's time for the data. Let's throw something in so we can see some results:

```
// purchase > $15 and <= $25
Purchase firstPurchase = new Purchase(new BigDecimal("16"), 1,
false);
FactHandle purchaseFact = session.insert(firstPurchase);
session.fireAllRules();
```

We've initialized a `Purchase` variable with an amount of $16, one taco, and no drink (man, that's an expensive taco!). If we refer back to our rules, we'll see that this should be enough to trigger our first rule. Notice the `fireAllRules()` function in there? We're executing now and should see some output from our rule consequence. Success! The console confirms that a discount of 10 percent has been added to our purchase:

```
Level 1 discount: 0.1
```

So our rules have done their thing and we're ready to close up shop. We finish up with a `catch` block that will relay any issues encountered, as well as dispose of the session:

```
} catch(Throwable t) {
    t.printStackTrace();
} finally {
    if (session != null) {
        session.dispose();
    }
}
```

What if we wanted to trigger our other rules as well? Let's add a few more lines to our test after the first call to `fireAllRules()` to flex the other two rules as well. You may have noticed we set something called a `FactHandle` at the same time we inserted a `Purchase` fact. We'll use that to update our rule session once we've made some changes to the `Purchase` object. Add these lines immediately after `fireAllRules()` and rerun the test:

```
System.out.println("---------------");

// purchase > $25
firstPurchase = new Purchase(new BigDecimal("26"), 1, false);
session.update(purchaseFact, firstPurchase);
session.fireAllRules();
System.out.println("---------------");

// combo purchase containing 3 tacos and a drink
firstPurchase = new Purchase(new BigDecimal("26"), 3, true);
session.update(purchaseFact, firstPurchase);
session.fireAllRules();

Level 1 discount: 0.1
---------------
Level 2 discount: 0.15
---------------
Level 2 discount: 0.15
Combo discount: 0.2
```

Congratulations! You're now working with Drools rules. If you'd like to download the accompanying code for this book (which includes better format and comments!) you can find it at http://www.packtpub.com/.

Top 5 features you need to know about

Let's discuss some of the more useful features of Drools and how to accomplish a few common tasks that you'll find yourself needing time and time again. We'll also discuss the five core modules that make up Drools so that when you're ready to expand your horizons and dig deeper into what Drools can do for you, you'll know what you're looking for.

Reading and writing Drools Rule Language syntax

Until now, we've only discussed the syntax of rules to the point of getting us off the ground. To continue working with the Drools Rule Language, there's more about the syntax you'll need to know and understand. To start off, let's reexamine a few of the basics we've seen thus far.

Some basics we've used

By now, hopefully I've nailed home the construct of when-then conditions. I think it's important to note here that while the taco shop rules we worked with were quite simple in nature, rules conditions can actually be very complex, meaning a rule may have more than one pattern. The syntax for each is basically the same:

```
Purchase ( $t : total > 15 )
```

This condition consists of a type, `Purchase`, a property that we're accessing, `total`, which we're binding to a variable, `$t`, and a Boolean evaluation on that property checking that the total of the purchase is greater than 15. Constraints can be made up of anything that evaluates to a true or false, or a Boolean value. Here we've done a simple "greater than" check, but patterns can also include Boolean properties, method calls, or other more complex Boolean expressions. Now's also a good time to point out that variables can either be bound to properties of an object, or the entire object itself:

```
rule "example rule"
when
   Purchase ( $t : total )
  $p :  Purchase ( total > $t )
then
   System.out.println("amount " + $p.getTotal() + " > " + $t);
end
```

As seen here, variables can be accessed in both, a condition and consequence of a rule. If used within a condition, the variable must have been declared and bound previously, and must be used on the right-hand side of the evaluator (that is you'll always use the order property, operator, then variable), otherwise our rule would expect that `Purchase` has a method `get$t()` to call, which would cause an exception to be thrown.

Some basics we haven't seen yet

In order to introduce a few additional things you'll want to be familiar with, let's consider this example rule file:

```
package org.tacoshop

import org.tacoshop.model.Purchase

global int comboCount

// hey here's a rule!
rule "example rule"
when
    $p : Purchase ( tacoCount >= comboCount, ( tacoCount % 2 == 0 ) )
then
    /* this consequence is pretty simple,
       but let's give it a comment anyways */
    $p.setDiscount(addDiscount($p, 0.15));
end

function double addDiscount(Purchase p, double discount) {
    return (p.getDiscount + discount);
}
```

We're familiar with the package declaration and import syntax, nothing new there. However, we've not seen a global variable declaration yet. Normally in programming, the term "global variable" has been engrained into our minds as a bad thing, but with Drools that's not the case. Global variables are tied to our rule session, meaning they're only global within limitation and available inside all of our rule conditions and consequences. In the previous code, we've referenced the global comboCount variable inside of a constraint to check if we've bought enough tacos to qualify for a combo discount. So where did the value of comboCount come from? Our rule session provides us with methods for handling globals similar to those we have for facts. To get a value in there, we'd want to call session.setGlobal("comboCount", 2) prior to executing our rules with fireAllRules(). If we didn't set a value beforehand, Drools would throw an exception. Also keep in mind that globals should be immutable as to avoid any surprises in unexpected behavior.

Another new concept I've demonstrated in this file is commenting. Any good code should include comments. Rules files can often grow to be very complex and should be no exception. DRL files allow single-line comments using either the # or // prefix, as well as multi-line comments using the /* comment */ construct.

If you take a closer look at the rule condition, you'll notice that we've formed an evaluative statement checking that the number of tacos in the purchase is evenly divisible by two. We're able to use any Java expression within a pattern as part of the condition, so long as the return is a Boolean value contributing to the truth of that condition.

Lastly, notice the function declared in this file. Functions within rule files carry the same functionality and syntax you'd expect from any Java class method, and we've referenced our function from within the rule consequence. If you find yourself repeating a lot of code, then a function can help to eliminate redundancy and simplify refactoring.

Rule attributes

Drools provides us with several ways to modify the behavior of a rule. Most are pretty complex in nature and beyond the scope of this book. We'll examine a few of the basic rule attributes here and recommend referring to the documentation later where the rest are covered in great detail. Rule attributes are added to the rule definition after the rule name, but before the when keyword.

+ `no-loop`: Sometimes a rule will modify a fact within the consequence and inadvertently cause a scenario where that exact same rule could fire again, starting an infinite loop. Using `no-loop` assures that the rule cannot trigger itself.

+ `salience`: We've already seen one example of `salience` in practice. It's used to determine the priority of a rule. By default, all rules have a `salience` of zero, but can be given a positive or negative value.

+ `dialect`: This specifies the syntax used in the rule. This can be specified per-rule, or it can be set on the package level and overridden on a per-rule basis. Currently, the options available are MVEL and Java.

Operators for constraints

Drools provides us with several operators for use within our rule constraints. Some of the most commonly used operators include the following:

+ `&&`: Both Booleans must be true. Previously we've used `&&` implicitly by including multiple property evaluations in a comma-separated series and by including multiple conditions:

```
Purchase ( tacoCount >= 2, discount < 0.15 )
Purchase ( total > 15 && tacoCount >= 2 )
```

+ `||`: One of the two Booleans must be true. Note that when using `&&` or `||` on a single property, the syntax can be shortened as follows:

```
Purchase ( total < 15 || total > 25 )
Purchase ( total < 15 || > 25 )
```

+ `( )`: We can form more complex patterns using parentheses:

```
Purchase ( ( total < 15 || > 25 ) && drinkIncluded )
```

+ `this`: This operator allows us to reference a fact within the condition of the pattern, which, among other uses, will disallow the same fact from satisfying multiple conditions:

```
$p : Purchase ( total > 15 )
Purchase ( this != $p, tacoCount > 2 )
```

◆ `in`: This checks if a value exists within a comma-separated list of values for potentially matching (can be paired with `not`):

```
Person ( name in ("Steve", "James", "Everett") )
Person ( name not in ("Jane", "Becca", "Mary") )
```

◆ `matches`: This matches against a regular expression (can be paired with `not`):

```
Person ( name matches "^[abc]" )
Person ( name not matches "^[xyz]" )
```

◆ `memberOf`: This checks if a field exists within a collection (can be paired with `not`):

```
Child ( name memberOf $niceList )
Child ( name not memberOf $naughtyList )
```

◆ `contains`: This is much like `memberOf`, but allows us to check the inverse—that a collection field contains a value (can be paired with `not`):

```
NiceList ( names contains $childName )
NaughtyList ( names not contains $childName )
```

◆ Common operators that are likely to be familiar to you from Java are ==, !=, >, >=, <, <=, and so on

Conditional elements for patterns

There are also a handful of conditional elements that you should be aware of which allow for a more complex usage of patterns:

◆ `exists`: At least one matching fact exists:

```
exists Purchase ( total > 15 )
```

◆ `not`: no matching facts exist:

```
not Purchase ( total > 15 )
```

◆ `from`: Allows access to nested collections:

```
$school : School ( )
Student ( name == "Joe" ) from $school.students
```

◆ `collect`: Allows evaluation of multiple facts within the system as a group:

```
$maleStudents : ArrayList ( )
    from collect ( Student ( gender == "male" ) )
```

◆ `accumulate`: Functions similarly to `collect` in that we're grouping facts, but also allows for manipulation on the collection prior to returning the result:

```
$savings : Number ( )
    from accumulate ( PiggyBank ( $total : total ),
                          sum ( $total ) )
```

✦ `eval`: Allows for execution of any block that returns a Boolean value. Please note that `eval` elements are not kind on engine performance and thus should only be used when absolutely necessary.

```
eval ( isTheSame ( $a, $b ) )
```

✦ `forall` (single): All facts of a given type match all the patterns supplied:

```
forall ( Student ( age >= 7 ) )
```

✦ `forall` (multi): All facts matching the first pattern must also match remaining patterns:

```
forall ( $dog : Dog ( breed == "dachshund" )
   Dog ( this == $dog, color == "red" ) )
```

✦ `and`: Both patterns must be true. Previously we've used `and` implicitly by including multiple conditions, but these can also be grouped with parentheses:

```
( Purchase ( tacoCount >= 2, discount < 0.15 )
   and Purchase ( total > 15 && tacoCount >= 2 ) )
```

✦ `or`: One of the two patterns must be true:

```
( Purchase ( total < 15 || total > 25 )
   or Purchase ( total < 15 || > 25 ) )
```

While I feel that these lists serve as a good basis for understanding various usages within DRL, note that it's not a list of all possible functionalities you will encounter in rules. For example, some words shown here, such as `not`, might be found within a constraint as a negation operator as well as outside of a pattern as shown in the previous example. As with any good software, Drools is also an ever-changing technology with a development team working hard to bring new functionalities to us with every release, so it's also safe to assume that new operators and conditional elements will be introduced. That being said, learning to yield those functionalities we just listed should provide for a very strong basis to author multitudes of business rules you'll find yourself in need of.

Working with facts

As we learned previously, rules engines reason over logic and facts. Logic, or in our case rules, serve as the bits of knowledge we know while facts serve as the objects that we're considering. Thus far, the rules and sessions we've worked with have been fairly simple. We defined some basic rules, loaded up a session, fired the rules, and that's it. In practice, knowledge bases will often grow in complexity and sessions will grow in size as we add more facts. The eventual need may arise for long living sessions and the ability to alter, add, or remove facts from the session. Drools allows us all of these capabilities. Let's take a look.

Manipulating facts in code

We've already seen how we insert a fact into a session from our executable code using
`session.insert(fact)`. However, if we need to modify or remove that fact from the
session later, then we'll need a reference to correlate our changes to the proper object in
memory. For this, Drools provides us with `FactHandle`:

```
Person person = new Person();
FactHandle personHandle = session.insert(new Person());
```

With a handle such as this, we could go on with our code, call various code blocks that alter
our `Person` object, then update the object in session memory so that the two are in sync:

```
person.setGender("female");
session.update(personHandle, person);
```

If, for some reason, we decide in our code that we no longer want `person` to be reasoned
over, then we could use our `FactHandle` to remove the `Person` object from the session's
working memory:

```
session.retract(personHandle);
```

Manipulating facts in rules

As your rules become more evolved, the ability to perform similar fact manipulation actions
from within rule consequences becomes desirable. Since rules operate within the realm of
the session, we are no longer on the outside peering in and don't need to use fact handles to
reference our objects. Inserting a fact from within a consequence looks like this:

```
then
    insert ( new Person() );
end
```

In order to alter a fact from within a rule consequence, you'll find that there are two options
available to you, `modify` and `update`. Though similar in concept, there's one very important
difference between the two. When you use `modify`, the fact is altered and the engine is
notified at the same time, preventing a gap between the two steps that could potentially lead
to indexing issues with the engine. `Update`, on the other hand, does not provide this same
functionality, so it is recommended that from within a rule consequence, you always use
`modify`. The syntax is as follows:

```
then
    modify( $person ) { setMood( "happy" ) };
end
```

And lastly, we can also remove a fact from working memory from within a rule consequence. `Retract` is identical to its code equivalent, except instead of passing a fact handle, we work directly with the fact itself:

```
then
   retract ( $person );
end
```

Testing your rules

Once you've put the work into developing a nice starter set of rules, you're going to want to make sure that as you develop more rules or change application behavior, what you've defined so far continues to do the job originally intended. By writing tests against rules, we can not only ensure their integrity, but also offer a roadmap of sorts to others who may want to examine how the rules behave and flag problem points when things have been refactored to a point of altering rule behavior. So how do we go about testing our rules? We'll use JUnit tests, much like the one we used previously to create a session for our taco shop rules. However, we can improve greatly upon the structure of our test class and do much more than just run a rule set. Let's start with defining our `@Before` and `@After` methods, both aptly named as JUnit will run them before and after each test method, respectively. We'll also go ahead and define a helper method to load up our rules using the same approach we did before.

```java
public class UsefulRuleTest {

    private KnowledgeBase knowledgeBase;

    private StatefulKnowledgeSession session;

    @Before
    public void setUp() {

      try {
         // load a new knowledgeBase with our rules
         knowledgeBase = populateKnowledgeBase();

         // initialize a session for usage
         session = knowledgeBase.newStatefulKnowledgeSession();

      } catch ( Exception e ) {
        e.printStackTrace();
          Assert.fail( e.getMessage() );
      }
    }
```

```
@After
public void tearDown() {

  // if session exists, dispose of it for GC
  if ( session != null ) {
    session.dispose();
  }
}

private KnowledgeBase populateKnowledgeBase() {

    // seed a builder with our rules file from classpath
    KnowledgeBuilder builder = KnowledgeBuilderFactory.
newKnowledgeBuilder();
    builder.add(ResourceFactory.newClassPathResource("discountRules.
drl"), ResourceType.DRL);
    if (builder.hasErrors()) {
        throw new RuntimeException(builder.getErrors().toString());
    }

    // create a knowledgeBase from our builder packages
    KnowledgeBase knowledgeBase = KnowledgeBaseFactory.
newKnowledgeBase();
    knowledgeBase.addKnowledgePackages(builder.
getKnowledgePackages());

    return knowledgeBase;
  }
}
```

Our setup method simply calls off to our helper method to get a knowledge base, then gets a session based on the knowledge base created. Notice that we're using the same rule set established for our taco shop scenario, `discountRules.drl`. The clean-up method checks if our session needs disposal, because as we mentioned before, we always want to ensure we free up session resources for proper garbage collection when we're done. So now that we have a shell to work with, let's start by adding a test that exercises two of our rules so that we can verify that no exceptions are incurred during rule compilation or execution:

```
@Test
public void testRulesCauseNoExceptions() throws Exception {

  // should trigger our first and last rule
  session.insert(new Purchase(new BigDecimal("16"), 2, true));

  Assert.assertEquals(2, session.fireAllRules(50));
  }
```

We've added a purchase that should satisfy the conditions for our purchase total between $15 and $25 and combo rules. To end the test, we've asserted two rules executed, as `fireAllRules()` will return the number of rules fired. Notice that unlike before, we've passed a parameter to `fireAllRules()` of 50. This number, when provided, indicates the maximum number of rule executions a session is allowed to perform before it stops and returns control to the calling code. The purpose of this is to handle infinite loops that may have been accidentally introduced in the rules. Without having some break-away mechanism, our thread would never end without intervention, thus it would not return to the test to fail the assertion.

As you can imagine, once you have a multitude of rules in place, the practice of getting tests to exercise a specific group and not triggering others becomes a tricky process. Rather than trying to balance these ever-changing expectations, we can selectively allow rules to fire, which means we can guarantee that only a single or specified set of rules will be exercised within a test. We do this using an implementation of `AgendaFilter`, which is a single-method interface we can use to filter out the rules we'll allow to fire. Let's add a class that will allow us to specify what rules we'd like to allow per test:

```
class CustomAgendaFilter implements AgendaFilter {

  private List<String> rulesToAllow;

  public CustomAgendaFilter(String[] ruleNames) {
    this.rulesToAllow = Arrays.asList(ruleNames);
  }

  public boolean accept(Activation activation) {
    if (this.rulesToAllow.contains(activation.getRule().getName()))
{
      return true;
    } else {
      return false;
    }
  }
}
```

We've set up a custom implementation of `AgendaFilter` with a constructor that accepts a string array of rule names that should be allowed to fire. The method that we need to extend, `accept()`, simply checks each activation's rule against the list of rule names, and if present, allows it to continue. Let's run a test with a `Purchase` variable identical to our first test that triggered two rules, but let's put our new filter to use and assert that only one rule fires:

```
@Test
public void testOnlyComboRuleFires() throws Exception {

  session.insert(new Purchase(new BigDecimal("16"), 2, true));
```

```
          String[] expectedRules = {"purchase contains combo"};
          Assert.assertEquals(1, session.fireAllRules(new CustomAgendaFilter
      (expectedRules)));
        }
```

Running this test will show that we did indeed trigger one and only one rule, but how can we be sure that it was the rule we intended to run? Well, the filter does the work for us here, but should we need to confirm rule names for any other reason or check the order in which multiple rules fired, we'd need a different approach. Before we get too far removed from filtering by rule name, it's worth mentioning that Drools provides a few filters for us to match single rules by various means:

+ `RuleNameEndsWithAgendaFilter`

+ `RuleNameEqualsAgendaFilter`

+ `RuleNameMatchesAgendaFilter`

+ `RuleNameStartsWithAgendaFilter`

Now for a final example; let's put a custom `AgendaEventListener` implementation into practice that will help solve our dilemma of asserting rule names and order. Here's our new class:

```
      class CustomAgendaEventListener implements AgendaEventListener {

          private List<String> rulesFired = new LinkedList<String>();

          public List<String> getRulesFired() {
            return this.rulesFired;
          }

          public void afterActivationFired(AfterActivationFiredEvent event)
      {
              rulesFired.add(event.getActivation().getRule().getName());
          }

          }
      }
```

There are many more methods that we must override in order to implement this interface, but for brevity, I've only included here what's important for this example. In real use, all other overridden methods could just have empty bodies. Now here's our test:

```
      @Test
        public void testVerifyRulesViaListener() throws Exception {

            CustomAgendaEventListener listener = new
      CustomAgendaEventListener();
```

```
    session.addEventListener(listener);

    // should trigger our first and last rule
    session.insert(new Purchase(new BigDecimal("16"), 2, true));

    Assert.assertEquals(2, session.fireAllRules(50));
    Assert.assertEquals(listener.getRulesFired().get(0), "purchase
over 15 and less than 25 dollars");
    Assert.assertEquals(listener.getRulesFired().get(1), "purchase
contains combo");
    }
```

We've built our custom listener, attached it to the session, and inserted a fact that we know should trigger two rules. Using our listener, we can assert that not only were the two rules that fired exactly the ones that we anticipated, but also that they've fired in the order we expected due to their salience levels.

Debugging the rule evaluation process

Maurice Wilkes, 1967 Turing award recipient, said the following:

> *"As soon as we started programming, we found to our surprise that it wasn't as easy to get programs right as we had thought. Debugging had to be discovered. I can remember the exact instant when I realized that a large part of my life from then on was going to be spent in finding mistakes in my own programs."*

Debugging is a necessity in most programming constructs, and working with rules is no exception. There will come a time when you need to understand exactly what's happening in a rule session and why something did (or didn't) occur. Thankfully, there are tools available to us that will aid us in our efforts.

Debugging with the Eclipse plugin

If you're taking advantage of the Eclipse plugin provided for working with Drools, then you'll find that the debugging process has not been overlooked. If you've worked with breakpoints and debugging Java code within Eclipse before, the process is very similar when working with rules. Start by opening your rule file and placing breakpoints where you'd like execution to pause for you to examine the current state. Note that only breakpoints placed in rule consequences are valid. You can add them in two ways:

1. Double-click on the shaded bar (or the line number, if you have them enabled) next to the line where you'd like to place the breakpoint.

2. Right-click on the shaded bar or line number where you'd like to place a breakpoint and select **Toggle Breakpoint**.

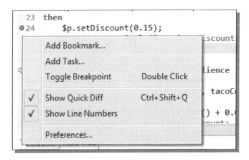

Now run your executable code as a Drools application by highlighting the method or class name, right-clicking on it, and navigating to **Debug As | Drools Application**. Execution should halt within your rule consequences at your breakpoints, provided the conditions for the rule have been satisfied and the rule has fired. Breakpoints placed in Java code will be respected as well, allowing us to examine what's happening both in and outside of rules in the same session.

Debugging with listeners

If you aren't using the Eclipse plugin, or perhaps you'd prefer to enhance your debugging by adding a bit of logging to allow for closer examination or auditing, then Drools also provides this capability. In order to better understand how we can do that, we first need to define a few things:

+ **Working memory**: Whenever we insert, modify, or retract a fact, we're adding, changing, or removing the instance within the working memory. You can think of working memory as the knowledge container; a place where all our facts reside.

+ **Agenda**: Drools benefits from excellent speeds partly due to the way the ReteOO algorithm is implemented. Without going into too much detail, we'll note that rather than waiting and making all considerations about our logic and data at the instant we give the go-ahead signal to fire rules, the engine does a portion of the work as facts are added, changed, and removed within the working memory. Since our rules are already known when we start to insert our data, the engine can go ahead and do some reasoning and determine, based on the new state of data, which rules would fire if nothing were to change between that point and our request to fire all rules. It does this by maintaining an agenda. When a rule's conditions are met based on the provided data, a rule activation is added to the agenda. If something changes causing that rule's conditions to no longer be satisfied, then the activation is removed from the agenda. When we finally get to the point that we call `fireAllRules()`, we're simply asking the engine to go down the list of activations currently on the agenda and trigger their consequences. Each time a fact is manipulated in working memory, the rule conditions are reconsidered and the agenda is updated appropriately.

✦ **Event listener**: Both the working memory and the agenda offer us the opportunity to take advantage of the observer pattern and attach special classes to our session that will be notified when certain events occur. These classes, called event listeners, offer us an excellent mechanism for passively debugging what's going on inside of our session.

Drools offers interfaces we can implement to customize event listeners for the working memory and the agenda. They are called, as you might expect, the `WorkingMemoryEventListener` and the `AgendaEventListener`. Each contain a series of methods that encapsulate all of the events potentially interesting to us when looking to debug or audit internal processes.

AgendaEventListener

You'll see methods within the `AgendaEventListener` that go beyond the scope of what's covered in this book, but in particular, take note of the following:

✦ `activationCancelled`

✦ `activationCreated`

✦ `beforeActivationFired`

✦ `afterActivationFired`

Using these four methods, we can monitor the session's agenda as we manipulate facts and cause activations to be added and removed. We can also detect the point in execution when rule consequences are about to be triggered, as well as the point directly after triggering has occurred.

Out of the box, Drools offers an implementation called `DebugAgendaEventListener` that implements every method of the interface in the same way: by printing the event captured to the `system.err` stream, which will provide us with a good deal of information about each event. This implementation will prove more than helpful when attempting to quickly take a look behind the scenes at what's going on with your rules.

WorkingMemoryEventListener

Inside the `WorkingMemoryEventListener`, there are fewer methods present than in the `AgendaEventListener`, and all are of interest to us. They are as follows:

✦ `objectInserted`

✦ `objectRetracted`

✦ `objectUpdated`

As the names imply, these capture events as facts are added, removed, and updated within working memory. Just as with the agenda listener, Drools has provided a debug implementation allowing detailed output about each event, the `DebugWorkingMemoryEventListener`.

Inference

Due to complexity, there's one additional functionality, inference, that I've withheld up to this point so that we would be better prepared with debugging and testing methods to fully dive in and understand the concept. Sometimes upon examining an object, we can infer some other piece of information that we may want to add to our rule session for the evaluation of further rules. Since this new information is closely related to the object, the information is typically only important as long as the object remains in session. When the object goes away, the new information is no longer valuable to us, and thus can also go away. Utilizing the support that Drools provides for inference, we can take some of the guess work out of tracking inferred relationships and reduce the amount of maintenance rules needed to remove an inferred fact when the related fact goes away. Let's start with a simple, non-inference example that we can build on and put some of what we've learned so far to use:

```
rule "fire detected, turn on alarm"
when
    Fire ( $r : room )
    Sprinkler ( room == $r, !on )
then
    System.out.println("fire detected, starting alarm!");
    insert( new Alarm($r) );
end

rule "alarm should turn on sprinklers, extinguishing fire"
when
    Alarm ( $r : room )
    $s : Sprinkler ( room == $r )
then
    System.out.println("alarm sounding, turning on sprinklers");
    modify( $s ){ setOn(true) };
end

rule "sprinkler came on, that puts out the fire"
when
    $f : Fire ( $r : room )
    Sprinkler ( room == $r, on )
then
    System.out.println("sprinklers put out the fire in " + $r);
    retract ( $f );
end

rule "fire's been put out, we should remove the alarm now"
when
    $a : Alarm ( $r : room )
    not Fire ( room == $r )
```

```
then
     System.out.println("fire's out, we can turn off the alarm now");
     retract ( $a );
end
```

Here we have a basic set of rules to take us through the simple steps of sounding an alarm for a fire, turning on the sprinklers, and removing the alarm when the fire is extinguished. Let's write up a test to show that our logic is sound. For brevity, the session initialization and the test structure have been omitted as we've seen them before; feel free to reference the accompanying code for this book, `FireAlarmTest.java`, to see the test in its entirety as well as the model POJOs in use:

```
// we need to indicate that room "kitchen" has a sprinkler in it
session.insert(new Sprinkler("kitchen"));

// now let's indicate that a fire has started in the kitchen
session.insert(new Fire("kitchen"));

// we expect all 3 of our rules to fire in this scenario
Assert.assertEquals(3, session.fireAllRules(50));

// fire's detected
Assert.assertEquals(listener.getRulesFired().get(0), "fire detected,
turn on alarm");

// sprinkler's turned on
Assert.assertEquals(listener.getRulesFired().get(1), "alarm should
turn on sprinklers, extinguishing fire");

// fire gets extinguished
Assert.assertEquals(listener.getRulesFired().get(2), "sprinkler came
on, that puts out the fire");

// and finally, we remove the alarm
Assert.assertEquals(listener.getRulesFired().get(3), "fire's been put
out, we should remove the alarm now");
```

Everything looks good. All of our assertions passed and we can see from our console output that things progressed as intended:

```
fire detected, starting alarm!
alarm sounding, turning on sprinklers
sprinklers put out the fire in kitchen
fire's out, we can turn off the alarm now
```

So, now examine what these rules look like when using inference. Let's change our first rule to use `insertLogical`, reading as follows:

```
rule "fire detected, turn on alarm"
when
    Fire ( $r : room )
    Sprinkler ( room == $r, !on )
then
    System.out.println("fire detected, starting alarm!");
    insertLogical ( new Alarm($r) );
end
```

Thanks to inference, we'll no longer have to keep up with removing the alarm ourselves, as it will be removed for us when the rule that initially put it in place is no longer satisfied. That means we can remove our last rule, "fire's been put out, we should remove the alarm now" entirely. Let's write another test that will exercise these rules and show that the alarm is removed from the session via inference:

```
// we need to indicate that room "kitchen" has a sprinkler in it
session.insert(new Sprinkler("kitchen"));

// now let's indicate that a fire has started in the kitchen
session.insert(new Fire("kitchen"));

// we expect all 3 of our rules to fire in this scenario
Assert.assertEquals(3, session.fireAllRules(50));

// fire's detected
Assert.assertEquals(listener.getRulesFired().get(0), "fire detected,
turn on alarm");

// sprinkler's turned on
Assert.assertEquals(listener.getRulesFired().get(1), "alarm should
turn on sprinklers, extinguishing fire");

// fire gets extinguished
Assert.assertEquals(listener.getRulesFired().get(2), "sprinkler came
on, that puts out the fire");

// assert that working memory contains only the sprinkler, meaning
alarm was removed
Assert.assertTrue( session.getObjects().size() == 1);
Assert.assertTrue( session.getObjects().toArray()[0] instanceof
Sprinkler);
```

The console output reflects what we've asserted that our three rules fire, and we've also asserted that the session only contains one object, a `Sprinkler`, meaning that the `Alarm` object was successfully removed from the session via inference.

```
fire detected, starting alarm!
alarm sounding, turning on sprinklers
sprinklers put out the fire in kitchen
```

There's one remaining caveat to using inference that I should mention before we move on. You'll need to ensure that your classes properly override the `equals` and `hashCode` methods in order to properly handle collisions between "equal" of both regularly and logically inserted facts.

The five core modules that make up Drools

Before we dive in, I need to confess a little white lie. These days, Drools only has four modules. The humanity! I know, I'm sorry. So why would I mislead you, the honest, caring, innocent reader into thinking there's five? Well, there used to be five, but one module turned into something much bigger. jBPM, having grown from the roots of the module once known as Drools Flow, has become a project of its very own. However, given that it's completely integrated with Drools and the two are often used together, I felt it very relevant and worthy of inclusion, so let's start there.

jBPM

Business Process Management (BPM) is a means of describing some process that occurs within your organization as a series of steps involved, how those steps are connected, and who is involved in performing them. jBPM, which is based on the BPMN 2.0 specification (a standard for graphical representation), serves as a tool for describing such processes in a flowchart format, giving visibility, clarity, and organization to processes that might otherwise be lacking. jBPM supports the entire process lifecycle, from development to execution and management up to retirement. Let's take a look at the graphical representation of a simple process.

Oscar's Oatmeal Cookies is a small successful business, delivering baked deliciousness worldwide. Its process is simple; whenever a new order is received, Oscar needs to bake some cookies, calculate and print an invoice, and ship the cookies out to the customer. The baking and invoicing cannot happen until an order is received and must be completed prior to shipping, but these two steps can possibly occur simultaneously. With jBPM, that process looks something like this:

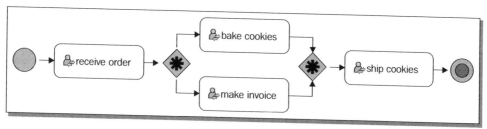

Drools Expert

By now we've learned quite a bit about what makes up rules, how to compile knowledge packages, and how to evaluate our rules with rule sessions. All the functionality that we've exercised in our examples belongs to the Expert module, which is the core engine of the system. We tell the engine about our logic and facts, and then we ask it to reason over what we've told it about and make some decisions for us. All other modules extend or rely upon the functionality of the core module, Expert.

Drools Fusion

Fusion gives the rules engine the ability to perform event processing, often referred to as **complex event processing (CEP)**. What's that, you say? Best to start with asking, "What is an event?" When something occurs in a point of time, that's an event. It may be instantaneous, or it may have a duration. What's important is that it has some temporal association. Using that definition of events, we can define CEP as the ability to take in masses of events, determine which are likely to be important, and figure out relationships and patterns between them. A proper example will go a long way in demonstrating what CEP is.

Ever got a call from your bank stating that some potentially fraudulent activity has been detected on your account? They're likely calling to verify a transaction or two with you as something suspicious has been flagged in their system. It could be something like an unusual amount, or maybe the transaction occurred outside of the geographical areas that you typically stay in. Your bank likely monitors massive amounts of transactions in a day. Each of these transactions is an event; something that occurred at a specific point in time. It's likely impossible for the bank to pore over each transaction manually and connect the dots and detect oddities in their records for every customer, so what is the best way to detect and overcome fraudulence? CEP to the rescue! By defining relationships between transactions that we're interested in, such as sudden spikes in amounts or purchases in two different countries within a short timeframe, the bank can feed all their incoming events into a rules engine and allow it to flag or notify someone when something seems a bit off.

Drools Guvnor

The Guvnor module provides us with a centralized repository with a layer of user authentication in which we can store and manage our rules, processes (like the one we just discussed), models, and other entities related to knowledge bases. Guvnor offers a collection of graphical editors with which we can view and edit our rules, and when combined with authentication, provides an excellent avenue for non-techie types to access and work with rules in a guided and controlled way. This allows us to bring the people with the domain expertise into the rule creation and maintenance processes. If you're worried that exposing your rules to business users creates a potential black hole in which rules could disappear forever, worry not! Guvnor provides versioning for all of our rules, so we'll not only be able to recover when necessary, but we'll also be able to audit the change trail and take steps to prevent future recurrences.

Drools Planner

Planner helps us (the name's a hint!) carry out automated planning. In order to optimize how we distribute and utilize resources in an organization, sometimes we need to consider multiple possible solutions and choose which works best for us. If Oscar's Oatmeal Cookies needs to make 100 deliveries in a day and only has 20 trucks to use, they'll probably want to figure out the best way to do it. While they could easily send out one truck to make all 100 stops, or all 20 trucks each with five stops each, these probably aren't the most effective options available. Instead, Oscar could plug his information into Planner, make some decisions about what factors are most important to him (for example, fuel cost versus number of stops any one truck must make) and let the rules engine figure out the optimal solution for his needs.

That's a wrap! Hopefully over the course of this book, I've armed you with the basics you need to get yourself started with Drools. We've only scratched the surface of syntax, features, and uses of Drools. There are many great resources out there when you're ready to start digging deeper, including some great reads from Packt Publishing and many blogs, tutorials, forums, and documentation available across the Internet. I implore you to check them out. Good luck and happy coding!

People and places you should get to know

If you need help with Drools, here are some people and places which will prove to be invaluable.

Official sites

- ✦ Homepage: `www.jboss.org/drools`
- ✦ Downloads: `www.jboss.org/drools/downloads`
- ✦ Documentation: `www.jboss.org/drools/documentation`
- ✦ Wiki: `community.jboss.org/wiki/JBossRules`
- ✦ Blog: `blog.athico.com`
- ✦ Source code: `github.com/droolsjbpm/drools`

Community

- ✦ Official mailing lists: `www.jboss.org/drools/lists`
- ✦ Official forum (mailing list archive): `drools.46999.n3.nabble.com/Drools-User-forum-f47000.html`
- ✦ Official IRC channel: `#drools, freenode.net`
- ✦ Intellifest, formerly known as Rulesfest, annual conference dedicated to reasoning technologies: `www.intellifest.org`
- ✦ Business Rules Forum, annual conference `www.businessrulesforum.com`
- ✦ Stack Overflow (always a helpful resource!): `www.stackoverflow.com/questions/tagged/drools`

Twitter

- ✦ Mark Proctor, Project Lead: `twitter.com/markproctor`
- ✦ Edson Tirelli, Fusion Lead: `twitter.com/edsontirelli`
- ✦ Geoffrey De Smet, Planner Lead: `twitter.com/geoffreydesmet`
- ✦ Toni Rikkola, Analysis Lead: `twitter.com/Rikkola`
- ✦ Mauricio Salatino, Drools and jBPM5: `twitter.com/salaboy`
- ✦ Drools Planner: `twitter.com/droolsplanner`
- ✦ Drools Guvnor: `twitter.com/droolsguvnor`
- ✦ jBPM: `twitter.com/jbossjbpm`
- ✦ Bob McWhirter, Founder: `twitter.com/bobmcwhirter`
- ✦ Michael Neale, Former Guvnor Lead: `twitter.com/michaelneale`
- ✦ For more open source information, follow Packt at `twitter.com/packtopensource`.

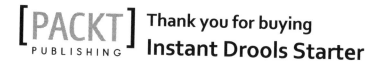

About Packt Publishing

Packt, pronounced 'packed', published its first book "*Mastering phpMyAdmin for Effective MySQL Management*" in April 2004 and subsequently continued to specialize in publishing highly focused books on specific technologies and solutions.

Our books and publications share the experiences of your fellow IT professionals in adapting and customizing today's systems, applications, and frameworks. Our solution based books give you the knowledge and power to customize the software and technologies you're using to get the job done. Packt books are more specific and less general than the IT books you have seen in the past. Our unique business model allows us to bring you more focused information, giving you more of what you need to know, and less of what you don't.

Packt is a modern, yet unique publishing company, which focuses on producing quality, cutting-edge books for communities of developers, administrators, and newbies alike. For more information, please visit our website: www.packtpub.com.

Writing for Packt

We welcome all inquiries from people who are interested in authoring. Book proposals should be sent to author@packtpub.com. If your book idea is still at an early stage and you would like to discuss it first before writing a formal book proposal, contact us; one of our commissioning editors will get in touch with you.

We're not just looking for published authors; if you have strong technical skills but no writing experience, our experienced editors can help you develop a writing career, or simply get some additional reward for your expertise.

JBoss Drools Business Rules

ISBN: 978-1-84719-606-4   Paperback: 304 pages

Capture, automate, and reuse your business processes in a clear English language that your computer can understand

1. An easy-to-understand JBoss Drools business rules tutorial for non-programmers

2. Automate your business processes such as order processing, supply management, staff activity, and more

3. Prototype, test, and implement workflows by themselves using business rules that are simple statements written in an English-like language

4. Discover advanced features of Drools to write clear business rules that execute quickly

Drools JBoss Rules 5.0 Developer's Guide

ISBN: 978-1-84719-564-7   Paperback: 320 pages

Develop rules-based business logic using the Drools platform

1. Discover the power of Drools as a platform for developing business rules

2. Build a custom engine to provide real-time capability and reduce the complexity in implementing rules

3. Explore Drools modules such as Drools Expert, Drools Fusion, and Drools Flow, which adds event processing capabilities to the platform

Please check **www.PacktPub.com** for information on our titles

Drools Developer's Cookbook

ISBN: 978-1-84951-196-4   Paperback: 310 pages

Over 40 recipes for creating a robust business rules implementation by using JBoss Drools rules

1. Master the newest Drools Expert, Fusion, Guvnor, Planner and jBPM5 features

2. Integrate Drools by using popular Java Frameworks

3. Part of Packt's Cookbook series: each recipe is independent and contains practical, step-by-step instructions to help you achieve your goal.

JBoss AS 7 Configuration, Deployment and Administration

ISBN: 978-1-84951-678-5   Paperback: 380 pages

Build a fully-functional, efficient application server using JBoss AS

1. Covers all JBoss AS 7 administration topics in a concise, practical, and understandable manner, along with detailed explanations and lots of screenshots

2. Uncover the advanced features of JBoss AS, including High Availability and clustering, integration with other frameworks, and creating complex AS domain configurations

3. Discover the new features of JBoss AS 7, which has made quite a departure from previous versions

Please check **www.PacktPub.com** for information on our titles

24746187R00030

Made in the USA
Lexington, KY
01 August 2013